Some Poems

R.g.morey

ISBN 978-93-5610-638-3

Published in India 2022 by Pencil

A brand of
One Point Six Technologies Pvt. Ltd.
123, Building J2, Shram Seva Premises,
Wadala Truck Terminal, Wadala (E)
Mumbai 400037, Maharashtra, INDIA
E connect@thepencilapp.com
W www.thepencilapp.com

Author biography

Blood covered her face
And flesh stuck in her nails
Her hair burnt dry thin
eyes dripping red and face pail
She is trying to speak
Her teeth are broken
Her tongue pulled out
She could not tell where she was taken
It was night when she was found
Her blood all around
Laying in mud
Crying on that ground
Her mother cried
No one stood with her
No one wrote her complain
No one fought for her
The girl died
Like they always do
No one noticed
No one knows she was who
Burnt girl was then forgotten
Even by her mother
No one cared or shed a tear when
There come new body and then another

CONTENTS

Little Flowers

Small and big flowers
Shining in sun scattering their beauty
You and I stood far, always then, together
And when I reached, alone, the land was gone
The lake we used to drink from
Water purest and cold and warm
You and I used to play barefoot
And now water is gone
White sky with so many shaped clouds
Birds flew singing passionately lullabies
You and I used to lay down on grass that hides underneath concrete now
But the sky is not white any more and I miss you
When I used to cry
You always ran to me
But now I can't see you
And you are gone, like everything else I loved
The deep forest and families of creatures
The flowing river and fresh rain
My family, my friends, my home, good food
And you are gone, like everything else I loved
Now I am crying again
But you are not here by my side to hold my hand
I can't breathe and the woman says, I will meet you soon
I am happy, but the pain won't let me smile

The sky is dark, darker than most morning
The wind is dustier, dustier than most days
The woman says, you have fresh air and good food, but I know you haven't eaten
You are waiting for me, like you used to do

Song

The song she sang
The way she danced
Her screams her tears her bloody face
Is still fresh in my memories
The book she used to read
Me laying on her lap
She running with one bad leg
Is still fresh in my memories
Her figths with me
when she wouldn't speak
Her last cry for help
Is still fresh in my memories
She never wished to be mine
Not till that night
When she was lost to all
And found by me
Her begging her prayers
The way she used to lie
Her body laying in my cage
Is still fresh in my memories
Police questioning to me
World crying for her, her face on TV
My envy for her
Is still fresh in my memories

The song she sang
The way she danced
Her screams her tears her bloody face
Is still fresh in my memories
The book she used to read
Me laying on her lap
She running with one bad leg
Is still fresh in my memories
Her figths with me
when she wouldn't speak
Her last cry for help
Is still fresh in my memories
She never wished to be mine
Not till that night
When she was lost to all
And found by me
Her begging her prayers
The way she used to lie
Her body laying in my cage
Is still fresh in my memories
Police questioning to me
World crying for her, her face on TV
My envy for her
Is still fresh in my memories
The song she sang
The way she danced
Her screams her tears her bloody face
Is still fresh in my memories
The book she used to read
Me laying on her lap
She running with one bad leg
Is still fresh in my memories

Her figths with me
when she wouldn't speak
Her last cry for help
Is still fresh in my memories
She never wished to be mine
Not till that night
When she was lost to all
And found by me
Her begging her prayers
The way she used to lie
Her body laying in my cage
Is still fresh in my memories
Police questioning to me
World crying for her, her face on TV
My envy for her
Is still fresh in my memories
The song she sang
The way she danced
Her screams her tears her bloody face
Is still fresh in my memories
The book she used to read
Me laying on her lap
She running with one bad leg
Is still fresh in my memories
Her figths with me
when she wouldn't speak
Her last cry for help
Is still fresh in my memories
She never wished to be mine
Not till that night
When she was lost to all
And found by me

Her begging her prayers
The way she used to lie
Her body laying in my cage
Is still fresh in my memories
Police questioning to me
World crying for her, her face on TV
My envy for her
Is still fresh in my memories
The song she sang
The way she danced
Her screams her tears her bloody face
Is still fresh in my memories
The book she used to read
Me laying on her lap
She running with one bad leg
Is still fresh in my memories
Her figths with me
when she wouldn't speak
Her last cry for help
Is still fresh in my memories
She never wished to be mine
Not till that night
When she was lost to all
And found by me
Her begging her prayers
The way she used to lie
Her body laying in my cage
Is still fresh in my memories
Police questioning to me
World crying for her, her face on TV
My envy for her
Is still fresh in my memories

The song she sang
The way she danced
Her screams her tears her bloody face
Is still fresh in my memories
The book she used to read
Me laying on her lap
She running with one bad leg
Is still fresh in my memories
Her figths with me
when she wouldn't speak
Her last cry for help
Is still fresh in my memories
She never wished to be mine
Not till that night
When she was lost to all
And found by me
Her begging her prayers
The way she used to lie
Her body laying in my cage
Is still fresh in my memories
Police questioning to me
World crying for her, her face on TV
My envy for her
Is still fresh in my memories
The song she sang
The way she danced
Her screams her tears her bloody face
Is still fresh in my memories
The book she used to read
Me laying on her lap
She running with one bad leg
Is still fresh in my memories

Her figths with me
when she wouldn't speak
Her last cry for help
Is still fresh in my memories
She never wished to be mine
Not till that night
When she was lost to all
And found by me
Her begging her prayers
The way she used to lie
Her body laying in my cage
Is still fresh in my memories
Police questioning to me
World crying for her, her face on TV
My envy for her
Is still fresh in my memories
The song she sang
The way she danced
Her screams her tears her bloody face
Is still fresh in my memories
The book she used to read
Me laying on her lap
She running with one bad leg
Is still fresh in my memories
Her figths with me
when she wouldn't speak
Her last cry for help
Is still fresh in my memories
She never wished to be mine
Not till that night
When she was lost to all
And found by me

Her begging her prayers
The way she used to lie
Her body laying in my cage
Is still fresh in my memories
Police questioning to me
World crying for her, her face on TV
My envy for her
Is still fresh in my memories
The song she sang
The way she danced
Her screams her tears her bloody face
Is still fresh in my memories
The book she used to read
Me laying on her lap
She running with one bad leg
Is still fresh in my memories
Her figths with me
when she wouldn't speak
Her last cry for help
Is still fresh in my memories
She never wished to be mine
Not till that night
When she was lost to all
And found by me
Her begging her prayers
The way she used to lie
Her body laying in my cage
Is still fresh in my memories
Police questioning to me
World crying for her, her face on TV
My envy for her
Is still fresh in my memories

The song she sang
The way she danced
Her screams her tears her bloody face
Is still fresh in my memories
The book she used to read
Me laying on her lap
She running with one bad leg
Is still fresh in my memories
Her figths with me
when she wouldn't speak
Her last cry for help
Is still fresh in my memories
She never wished to be mine
Not till that night
When she was lost to all
And found by me
Her begging her prayers
The way she used to lie
Her body laying in my cage
Is still fresh in my memories
Police questioning to me
World crying for her, her face on TV
My envy for her
Is still fresh in my memories
The song she sang
The way she danced
Her screams her tears her bloody face
Is still fresh in my memories
The book she used to read
Me laying on her lap
She running with one bad leg
Is still fresh in my memories

Her figths with me
when she wouldn't speak
Her last cry for help
Is still fresh in my memories
She never wished to be mine
Not till that night
When she was lost to all
And found by me
Her begging her prayers
The way she used to lie
Her body laying in my cage
Is still fresh in my memories
Police questioning to me
World crying for her, her face on TV
My envy for her
Is still fresh in my memories
The song she sang
The way she danced
Her screams her tears her bloody face
Is still fresh in my memories
The book she used to read
Me laying on her lap
She running with one bad leg
Is still fresh in my memories
Her figths with me
when she wouldn't speak
Her last cry for help
Is still fresh in my memories
She never wished to be mine
Not till that night
When she was lost to all
And found by me

Her begging her prayers
The way she used to lie
Her body laying in my cage
Is still fresh in my memories
Police questioning to me
World crying for her, her face on TV
My envy for her
Is still fresh in my memories
The song she sang
The way she danced
Her screams her tears her bloody face
Is still fresh in my memories
The book she used to read
Me laying on her lap
She running with one bad leg
Is still fresh in my memories
Her figths with me
when she wouldn't speak
Her last cry for help
Is still fresh in my memories
She never wished to be mine
Not till that night
When she was lost to all
And found by me
Her begging her prayers
The way she used to lie
Her body laying in my cage
Is still fresh in my memories
Police questioning to me
World crying for her, her face on TV
My envy for her
Is still fresh in my memories

The song she sang
The way she danced
Her screams her tears her bloody face
Is still fresh in my memories
The book she used to read
Me laying on her lap
She running with one bad leg
Is still fresh in my memories
Her figths with me
when she wouldn't speak
Her last cry for help
Is still fresh in my memories
She never wished to be mine
Not till that night
When she was lost to all
And found by me
Her begging her prayers
The way she used to lie
Her body laying in my cage
Is still fresh in my memories
Police questioning to me
World crying for her, her face on TV
My envy for her
Is still fresh in my memories
The song she sang
The way she danced
Her screams her tears her bloody face
Is still fresh in my memories
The book she used to read
Me laying on her lap
She running with one bad leg
Is still fresh in my memories

Her figths with me
when she wouldn't speak
Her last cry for help
Is still fresh in my memories
She never wished to be mine
Not till that night
When she was lost to all
And found by me
Her begging her prayers
The way she used to lie
Her body laying in my cage
Is still fresh in my memories
Police questioning to me
World crying for her, her face on TV
My envy for her
Is still fresh in my memories
The song she sang
The way she danced
Her screams her tears her bloody face
Is still fresh in my memories
The book she used to read
Me laying on her lap
She running with one bad leg
Is still fresh in my memories
Her figths with me
when she wouldn't speak
Her last cry for help
Is still fresh in my memories
She never wished to be mine
Not till that night
When she was lost to all
And found by me

Her begging her prayers
The way she used to lie
Her body laying in my cage
Is still fresh in my memories
Police questioning to me
World crying for her, her face on TV
My envy for her
Is still fresh in my memories

When we meet

When the dark sky will be clean
The water in the river will be ours
And our fields free of dust and bodies
Then we shall go to the fair together
Tiny lights everywhere like stars hung on doors
You me and all of our gang
Playing all games the fair has to offer
Humming songs and eating sweets
We will have that all once again I promise
Once the blood is dried on the ground
Once the enemy is claimed and the flag has risen
When this all is gone then we can be together
When the rumbling of those tanks comes
My heart sinks and my hands shake
But I remember what is there if I loose
And I can't let them touch my fields, my people and you
Each night we sing songs even when we lose one or two
The anthem truly fuels my heart with warmth and pride
Pride that, we did not start this chaos
Pride that the dark shadow of the enemy is frightful of its destiny
When I come back I promise the world will be better
Fewer things to be afraid of and more reasons to smile at
When I come back I hope to see you smiling
And ask for your hand in front of the town

When this war is over history will have one more scar
Fields, where we fought, will be useless
Wells will be filled with heads men
And if I live there is going to be both pain and pride attached to me for all eternity

Poor

Her name I learnt
By walking through shadows
Her voice I heard
From under the bridge
She walks through the garden to pick flowers
I glimpse at her from the working field
She smiles at everyone as she walks through the market
I follow her carrying the goods of others
When at night I rest by the river
I can hear her sing in her bungalow
My heart is too dirty for her
Her hands are too soft for life with me
She will never be mine and I will be of hers
That's that and nothing else

She

I still think about her
I still think of her hair
Her smile her giggles
Her soft and tender chicks
I still miss her
Going on walks with her
Watching her as she smiles
Looking for a chance to show her that I care
But she is no more
Changed into someone I hate
I change into someone she hates
And life has moved on
But day and again she comes to mind
Foggy image of her still fresh
Mesmerising sent still in the air
But she is long gone and that's life as I know
If she were her lips would have been on mine
Out finger intertwined
Our breaths heavy and she whispere in my ears
Our lives had blossomed but no
She is gone
Long gone into a world full of unknowns

Dreams

In the dreams of a distant land
In the dreams of peace and love
In the dreams of truth and adventure
In the dream of a place that is ours
In that dream I see you
In that dream, our feet ripple the ocean
In that dream, the time has stopped
In that dream I see you smile
In that dream, your hand is in mine
In that dream, everything is quite
And I asked you to be mine
But dream ends and everything with it

Dark

In the dark distant night
When owls fly and the wolves howl
When the moon is hiding in clouds and tiny creatures roam for their pray
When it is that quiet that deafens
Then there is fear and fear alone in the hearts of most men
Tightening their feast and tears in their eyes
There is worry in their eyes
Not mine
My heart is filled with love for you
So much so that I am never alone
When the night has become like the reaper
I smile instead
Cause at a far distance I can see you chuckling

Hue

There are very
Few of wonders I think of
Flower's amazing hue
Morning's beautiful dew
Nature, gardens, sky to name a few
But most importantly you

Ghost in my room

Ghost came into my room
Said my time was coming soon
I wasn't scared, it was a girl
I knew it wasn't my time yet, that goon
Her face was cut in the middle
There a bunch of hair in the right hand
A person's ear in her left
Her feet were dirty covered in sand
I took my blanket over my head
And slept like a child
She pulled my blanket away and screamed
Her hairs were standing her jaw fallen
I put fingers in my ears and dreamed
Her long nail hand she put on my face
With other, she pulled my hair up
Now that I knew it was serious I got out
I tried to pull her hair, but, no luck
When I was out of the bed finally
She groaned at me in hate
Then she lay down on the bed and asked for a blanket
I slept on the couch as it was too late
Before she said, good night
She smiled in delight
And I could still get a priest
But I won't, all couples fight

Stand out

I can't stand out
It is so cold
But worriers are on protest on road
Because of some ass-holes
Nights are long
Full of mosquitoes when light goes out
But worriers are on protest at nights
Enraged they shout
When time is little hard most run
Here death is sentenced by law
But the worriers are on protest fearless
Because all seems be blind of the flaw

Blood

Blood covered her face
And flesh stuck in her nails
Her hair burnt dry thin
eyes dripping red and face pail
She is trying to speak
Her teeth are broken
Her tongue pulled out
She could not tell where she was taken
It was night when she was found
Her blood all around
Laying in mud
Crying on that ground
Her mother cried
No one stood with her
No one wrote her complain
No one fought for her
The girl died
Like they always do
No one noticed
No one knows she was who
Burnt girl was then forgotten
Even by her mother
No one cared or shed a tear when
There come new body and then another

Hell

Into the hell
Through the carrier of deaths
I travel
Moaning in pain
Out I see cannot
Eyes are bleeding
And darkness drank me in
Blood I drink, rotting flesh, is all I got
And now the flesh
I hinged to for so long
Will be part of the darkness
I will be lost in madness maze
I hear them
Part I cannot
They have rotting flesh and stinky blood
But their pain is not the same
The carrier will stop
And the end will be pleasing
Till the horror begins
And like my blood and flesh, my soul starts to rot

Child

It was a good morning for child
It was a morning for child
It was beginning of misery for child
It was day of hunger for child
Child woke up and had a blast, played and danced a lot
Child woken up by screams and blows on head
Child had a headache he was stripped and tied to bed
Child was begging he wanted a bun but nothing that morning he got
Child ride in a car AC music and smiles on face
Child was sent to school on foot after scolding
Child was begging crying to let go, the man did, but only as a game, to chase
Child was hit by a car he lay there, there was a wrapped bun coming out of his, unfolding
Child came home to smiling to find his family death
Child that night when parents were at fight again hung itself for life of his to end
Child was now strangled, his flesh was old, out of taste
Child could have been saved but he was three months too late

Rest

Let blood flow from eyes
Of the traitors to the land
And let their gut rote
On the red path of corpses
Let hunger drive them out
Of fake humanity they claim of
Let jungle rule be prevail
Let those unholy burn in hell
And when there is enough pain
Deafening screams and cries for pity
When there is no eye with hope in it
Then you can rest in peace

Bad and Good

Good has and so has the bad
Bad has and so has the good
Will pass, it will pass
Will pass, it will pass
Hope was crushed, dreams shattered
Alone, dim, lost, thrown down
Bad and the good
Will pass, it will pass
Shattered being rose from ashes
Hope again rising from within
Bad and the good
Will pass, it will pass
Long story of last year
Gave way to the dreams for the next
Bad and the good
Will pass, it will pass
Wish of life that was distant
Is now nearer and joy dangling from lips
Bad and the good
Will pass, it will pass
Like joy once did, the pain too
Like sorrow, the smiles too
Like hope, the dismay too
Like bad, the good too

Like the good, the bad too
Will pass, it will pass

Let's Dance

Look the sky is falling
Look the floor is shaking
Look the life is funny, see me laugh
Look the wall is moving, still can't touch
Was that mine or yours
Was she mine ever, or it was a game
Was not that trip the best
Was not I your best friend then
It is empty again, who drank
It is raining I think, Nah! Maybe!?
It is her fault, not mine, you know
It is you who keep me happy man, give me a kiss
Find, I am done anyways
Fine, I am never going to meet her anyways
Fine, I am ready, where are we going
Fine, lets dance

Amazing nights

Nights are the loudest
If we can hear it
The cries the fights
Escaping foot follows the path still lit
Each step farther from screaming city
Lightened the brains and stops the thoughts
Children sleep daily at night
They know the screams won't stop
Roaring hero arises
In their dreams every night
Problem comes and monsters too
But children are brave and powerful to fight
Here at edge of the city cold wind blows
The fallen leaves off the street
Water flows underneath the bridge
And quite moon is yet whole new treat
Too far from everything
But eyes catches glims and voices are heard
The free ones are walking old and young
Migrating out of the city like a bird
A group smiles known faces
Heart gets heavier and head lighter
One smiles gently slipped hand into mine
And the night gets a little quitter
We walked slowly

To the moon big and shiny
We sat on green grass at the bank of the river
Looking at the big sky feeling so tiny

No one Cares

No one came
No hand to help me
When I fell down
Only talking mouths and laughs
No one trusted
No one wanted to
My dreams trash for others
My life game for all
No one clapped
On my first dance
My first twirl, my first jump
Mumbling gossips and praying eyes
No one came to stop
In this men's world
When I was forced against the wall
Laughing men strong arms and blades
No one had guts
No one could stop me
They tried, the world tried, men tried
But failed and I laughed, I laughed
No one leaves their seats
No one can take eyes off me
I dance, I twirl, I jump
They clap, they cheer my name, and I, like always don't care

Ripper

Ripper of the souls
Walked on earth
Amongst all mortals
To get the ones whose time has come
A mortal child
Innocent fibble
World to him is his mother still
His soul Ripper takes with no regrets
A man killed so many
Now his time has came
He is cold and weak
His soul ripper pull out with one hand
A woman on a path
Laying in her own blood
Mortals crying, mortals talking, mortals laughing
He takes her soul out gently
An old man on a soft bed
Saw the ripper coming and smiled
Finally, his time had come
Ripper extend a hand for the old man to hold
Ripper took all souls and carried them with him
In one bag he keeps them
All mortal differences and hates he did not let them carry
Ripper walks amongst mortal to collect souls

Will Pass

Good has and so has the bad
Bad has and so has the good
Will pass, it will pass
Will pass, it will pass
Hope was crushed, dreams shattered
Alone, dim, lost, thrown down
Bad and the good
Will pass, it will pass
Shattered being rose from ashes
Hope again rising from within
Bad and the good
Will pass, it will pass
Long story of last year
Gave way to the dreams for the next
Bad and the good
Will pass, it will pass
Wish of life that was distant
Is now nearer and joy dangling from lips
Bad and the good
Will pass, it will pass
Like joy once did, the pain too
Like sorrow, the smiles too
Like hope, the dismay too
Like bad, the good too

Like the good, the bad too
Will pass, it will pass

Family

Small and big flowers
Shining in sun scattering their beauty
You and I stood far, always then, together
And when I reached, alone, the land was gone
The lake we used to drink from
Water purest and cold and warm
You and I used to play barefoot
And now water is gone
White sky with so many shaped clouds
Birds flew singing passionately lullabies
You and I used to lay down on grass that hides underneath concrete now
But the sky is not white any more and I miss you
When I used to cry
You always ran to me
But now I can't see you
And you are gone, like everything else I loved
The deep forest and families of creatures
The flowing river and fresh rain
My family, my friends, my home, good food
And you are gone, like everything else I loved
Now I am crying again
But you are not here by my side to hold my hand
I can't breathe and the woman says, I will meet you soon
I am happy, but the pain won't let me smile

The sky is dark, darker than most morning
The wind is dustier, dustier than most days
The woman says, you have fresh air and good food, but I know you haven't eaten
You are waiting for me, like you used to do

My Mental struggles

Bored and tired
Mental health had getten me fully
Dead is shaking
And dizziness is griping
Dead would have been a path
But life is not that easy
As it was easy few years ago

Budget

Love partner is like mobile
You want her
Like her
Accept all the changes she chose
Ready to spent time with her
Ready to spend money on her
Like the touch of her
Like the appearance
And can't live without her
Of course only till new mobile comes in the market that is in your budget

Agony

Let blood flow from eyes
Of the traitors to the land
And let their gut rote
On the red path of corpses
Let hunger drive them out
Of fake humanity they claim of
Let jungle rule be prevail
Let those unholy burn in hell
And when there is enough pain
Deafening screams and cries for pity
When there is no eye with hope in it
Then you can rest in peace

With Blood and Tears

A photo was put
A glamorous one
And eyes saw that smile
And that charm
Those words that spoke
Of nothing but self Pity
Shone like sun
In eyes of many
And the photo was glorified
Name became sacred
And followers became violent
Photo earned and grew
Smile was glowing and name was famous
Words spoke nothing of what pain is
World was forgotten in those words
That the photo har written
Faceless message that flew from unknown
Was suned and thrown away
Truth and logic
That only faceless knows
Are forgotten and over looked
And the charmis photos
Took mass as their slaves
And worlds just followed
One who looks nice

Talk nice
And forgot themselves
Forgot the words
Words that faceless writes
With blood and tears

Creatures

Dark eyed beast
Blood red teeth
Shadowy night fell upon
Dark creatures had their dawn
They danced around
Howled and shouted empting the surround
That dark night moon was shy
Bats flew in dark sky up high
When clock had its twelfth bell
Creatures woke up in from pit dark as hell
All these big and alive creatures
Who had scary haunting features
Came together
Danced and sang together
Night was their time
To be free, safe, smile and rhyme
But time changed quickly
And real monsters appeared
Men came with their guns
And the creatures were, forever, disappeared

Mother

So little was there to spare
But still yet again
She did
And suffered her hunger
She did not cry
Or cursed lord for her pain
She watched her child sleep
And was happy yet again
Morning was another day
Work and toil and pain
She sweated and thought of her child
All day long , and child waited for food
When one night
She was on way
To see smile on her child 's face
As she had begged a bread out of store
But her way was cut
By man in uniform
She was held and striped and killed
And child of hers stayed hungry that night
He cried and slept
And days latter like most others
Disease and hunger succumbed him
And he saw his in clouds smiling yet again

Had a Dream

Had a dream
And she was there
Dancing and smiling and giggling
As always
And I was there looking
And her breathtaking image of life
And was lost of words and and thoughts
As always
She ran to me held my hand
Pulled me closer and we kissed
She blushed and kissed again
As always
I hugged her close and told her I love you
She started crying
Her body disappeared just her smell remained
As always
As always when I woke up
I was shaking and crying
I had my bottle left to drink from
And night to think of her
No night has past sense I lost her
That I don't think of her
But she cannot come back
And dreams are too real
That I fear to be stuck

I walked out into the cold into the fog
To look at the stars and moon
And to find her up there smiling at me
As always

And lost Her

Loved her lost her
She loved him
And lost
In tears she ran
On an empty street at night
Owls watched and bars laughed
Moon hid under the clouds
And rain poured on her red face
When finally she stopped
She fell down into mud
People crossed by giggled
And I saw her laying there
I got to her and smiled
Held her hand and took her with me
She bath and drank and slept
Next day was of crying again
Then when she was fine and happy
I thought to myself why not say it to her
That I loved her
When had built in enough of courage
She was with another man
He was charming and was rich
She loved him dearly
And I loved her
And lost her

And then she was gone (incomplete)

And there she was
Staring at me scared and lonely
Weak
Someone had hurt her not the body but in courage
Would she ever had been able to shine in the world again with her smile
I could have maybe helped her
But something held me back
It was a false future, with some weak bonds, little lack of courage and false
the truth I told myself
It was the honesty may be that I lack
Beaten up and scared left alone given many names
She ran, she cried, she begged
And there she was
Asking me for help, not her words just her eyes
I am hurt too, hurt myself, killed something within
Who was I to define who she was
Who was I to decide what she deserved
Who was I not to shield her from nationalist
I was no one, I am no one
She did not wrote her reason, why
She did not explained her life to the world
Alone she was, else she had stayed a little while in this mad place

Photos in news, discussion in panels, relatives gathered
And there she was
Hanged to the ceiling
And there she left
The world with no feeling
No reason, why?
No explanation
She just ended her life
Not weak, no, she was brave once, but it was before they
killed her innerself
And now she is gone
Few days passed by I saw a young angel
Tears she had, was crying red drops scared alone asking for
help I blinked once
And there she was

www.ingramcontent.com/pod-product-compliance
Lightning Source LLC
LaVergne TN
LVHW050423160726
843469LV00041B/1213

* 9 7 8 9 3 5 6 1 0 6 3 8 3 *